★ SPORTS STARS ★

TERRELL DAVIS
BRONCO BUSTER

BY CALEB MacLEAN

Children's Press®
A Division of Grolier Publishing
New York London Hong Kong Sydney
Danbury, Connecticut

Photo Credits

Photographs ©: AllSport USA: 39 (Al Bello), 29 (Vincent Laforet), 19 (Ken Levine), 33 (Doug Pensinger); AP/Wide World Photos: 47 (Ed Andrieski); Archive Photos: 3, 35 (Reuters/Mike Segar); Sports Illustrated Picture Collection: 10, 17, 44 left (Peter Read Miller); SportsChrome East/West: 12 (Vincent Manniello), 15, 44 right (Louis Raynor), cover (Tony Tomsic), 6, 30, 32 (Rob Tringali Jr.), 38 (Michael Zito);; Tom DiPace: 21, 26, 40, 43, 45, 46; University of Georgia: 22 (J. Cribb), 20 (R. O'Quinn).

Visit Children's Press® on the Internet at:
http://publishing.grolier.com

Library of Congress Cataloging-in-Publication Data

Maclean, Caleb.
  Terrell Davis, Bronco buster / by Caleb Maclean.
    p. cm. — (Sports stars)
    Summary: A biography of the star running back for the Denver Broncos, Terrell Davis.
    ISBN: 0-516-21663-5 (lib. bdg.)   0-516-27006-0 (pbk.)
    1. Davis, Terrell, 1972- —Juvenile literature. 2. Football players—United States Biography Juvenile literature. 3. Denver Broncos (Football team) Juvenile literature. [1. Davis, Terrell, 1972- . 2. Football players. 3. Afro-Americans Biography.] I. Title. II. Title: Terrell Davis. III. Series.
GV939.D347M33   1999
796.332'092—dc21
[B]—dc21   99-23009
                                               CIP
                                                AC

© 1999 by Children's Press®, A Division of Grolier Publishing Co., Inc.
All rights reserved. Published simultaneously in Canada.
Printed in the United States of America.
1 2 3 4 5 6 7 8 9 10 R 08 07 06 05 04 03 02 01 00 99

CONTENTS

CHAPTER 1
Cut-Back King 7

CHAPTER 2
Rough Start 9

CHAPTER 3
What Else Can Go Wrong? 17

CHAPTER 4
Sixth-Round Sensation 25

CHAPTER 5
A Super Season 31

CHAPTER 6
Back to Back 37

Chronology 44

Statistics 47

About the Author 48

CUT-BACK KING

Terrell Davis rumbles to his right behind a wall of blockers. He watches the defense move with him on the other side, waiting for someone to make a move. When three opponents overpower teammates to his left, the time seems right. Terrell turns upfield and suddenly explodes to his left—right into the teeth of the penetrating defense. He bursts through the surprised tacklers, who bounce off him like rag dolls.

Terrell's familiar "cut-back" move has worked again. Like a martial artist, he has used his opponents' own momentum against them, and now he is free to smash into the cornerbacks and safeties who converge to block his path. By the time they catch up to drag him down, he has carried the ball more than 30 yards.

Everyone who plays the Denver Broncos knows exactly what the team is going to do. What they do *not* know is how to stop Terrell Davis. Of course, he has been facing challenges for more than 20 years. And nothing has stopped him yet.

ROUGH START

Being a member of a big family has its good points and bad points. Terrell Davis was the youngest of six boys in his family. He loved the fact that he always had someone to play with, someone to look after him, and someone whom he could look up to. The bad times came after Terrell turned eight, when his mother and father could no longer live together. Kateree Davis often worked double-shifts as a nurse's aide. She even added college classes into her busy schedule. Joe Davis, on the other hand, drifted from job to job. And when he was not working, he sometimes got involved in illegal activities. Eventually, their marriage fell apart.

Terrell (left) and four of his brothers: Joe Jr., Reggie, Terry, and Bobby. Terrell was named after his mother's favorite singer, Tammy Terrell.

Kateree and her two oldest sons moved to an apartment a few blocks away, in San Diego, while Joe stayed put and looked after the four youngest boys. On the weekends, all of the kids would go over to Kateree's place, and Joe would disappear into the night. There were many scary moments living with Joe. He was often drunk or under the influence of drugs, and his behavior was dangerous and unpredictable. Once, Joe lined up Reggie, Bobby, Terry, and Terrell and aimed a pistol at them. He squeezed off four shots, each one slamming into the wall just above their heads.

Joe calmed down considerably after being diagnosed with Lupus, a muscular disorder. But even in his wildest moments, the boys never believed he would harm them. "I wasn't scared," Terrell claims. "I knew he wasn't going to kill us. He wouldn't do that. He loved us too much."

Terrell was very big for his age—as much as 20 pounds heavier than the other kids in his class. Eventually, he gravitated to football and became the star running back for his Pop Warner team. He often gained more than 300 yards a game. It usually took three or four boys to bring him down. The other kids called him "Boss Hogg," after a rotund character on the television show *Dukes of Hazzard*. He enjoyed being the center of attention. He liked it when others depended on him to carry the load.

Every time Terrell suits up, he knows he may suffer a painful migraine headache.

One evening after practice, while Terrell was waiting for his mother to pick him up, his eyes stopped working. Everything was hazy and scrambled. "I was like, *man*, I'm going blind," he remembers. Although Terrell's vision returned a few minutes later, by the time he got home, waves of pain began pounding in his head, and he felt nauseated. This episode lasted for more than six hours, and it was the most frightening experience of Terrell's young life. Terrell later learned that he was prone to migraine headaches, but early in his life, doctors did not know how to treat these painful episodes.

★ ★ ★

Terrell was a tough kid. He continued to play football despite his episodes. He also refused to follow his friends when they started hanging out in the streets and getting into trouble, which took just as much courage and determination. He rarely missed a day of school. Although he was not a straight-A student, he did his work and paid attention in class. When Terrell was 14, his father—who stubbornly refused to take his Lupus medicine—fell into a coma and died. After that, Terrell changed. "All life just came out of me," he says.

In a way, he just gave up. Terrell quit sports altogether and only attended school when he felt like it. When he did show up in class, he did his best to disrupt it. The teachers hated him. At night, he would wander into the darkness looking for something to take his mind off his troubles. His mom did not know if he would show up for breakfast or end up dead on some street corner.

★ ★ ★

The only tie to his old life that Terrell did not cut was his friendship with a boy named Jamaul Pennington. Kateree had taken Jamaul in when his mother could no longer afford to support him. Afterward, Jamaul and Terrell did everything together, and they began acting so much alike that people assumed they were related. One of the things the teenagers talked about was opening the coolest nightclub in San Diego. They had the whole project planned out—finding the space, designing the interior, choosing the music, and keeping the books. As Terrell began to drift away, Jamaul used their big plan to bring him back. He convinced Terrell that he had to graduate from high school and get professional business training in college. Eventually, Terrell saw that Jamaul was right. He agreed to dedicate himself to his studies, and he began playing football again.

Terrell knows how important school is. He nearly dropped the ball on his football career when he neglected his studies.

★ ★ ★

In 1988, Terrell transferred to Lincoln Prep for his junior year, and he went out for the football team that fall. He just wanted to make the squad—he did not care which position he played. So, when he saw more than a dozen boys competing for the running back slot, he looked for a less crowded position. A few days later, Terrell learned that he was Lincoln's new nose tackle. Later that year, he also took over as placekicker. Lincoln coach Vic Player knew there was more to Terrell than tackling and kicking. During the 1989 season, Player shifted Terrell to running back. He responded with more than 700 rushing yards, and the team made it all the way to the city championship game.

WHAT ELSE CAN GO WRONG?

Terrell was happy that he had decided to get serious about school. His mom was proud of him, too. He had some great football memories, and he had his high-school diploma. "I've done things wrong," he admits. "I'm not an angel. But you can control your life. You can turn it around."

The question was, now that he had turned it around, where should he go next? Jamaul

Terrell is as proud of his mother as she is of him.

★ ★ ★

decided to join the Navy to learn some of the technical skills he would need when they began building their nightclub. Terrell thought about the military—his two oldest brothers had joined—but was not sure he would like it. College seemed like a good idea, but it was very expensive. Because Terrell had missed two entire seasons of high-school ball, no college teams wanted to offer him a scholarship.

Luck, however, was on Terrell's side. A couple of hours north, the coaches at Long Beach State University were concerned about their lack of running backs. Terrell's half-brother, Reggie Webb, played for them and mentioned that there was a great back down at Lincoln Prep. No one knew about him, Reggie explained, because he had only played the position for one season. Coach George Allen—who had a reputation for finding "hidden treasures"—contacted Terrell and invited him to try out. Impressed with what

Long Beach State coach George Allen. He saw potential in Terrell that no one else did.

he saw, the coach offered Terrell a scholarship. Not until later did Allen discover that Reggie was Terrell's half-brother!

The thought of playing in front of huge crowds at Sanford Stadium (above) convinced Terrell to go to Georgia.

Unfortunately, after Terrell played at Long Beach State for just one season, the school decided to shut down its football program. Terrell would be allowed to transfer to another school and continue playing football, or stay in Long Beach as a student. A few colleges expressed interest, including the University of Georgia, which was almost 3,000 miles away. Terrell visited Georgia and was impressed with the reception he got. The team really seemed to want him. Terrell decided to accept Coach Ray Goff's offer and made it official. He was now a Georgia Bulldog. "What really impressed me about Georgia was the facilities," he remembers. "I thought, 'Wow, it would be great to play before 85,000 people.' Remember, I was used to playing in front of 5,000 fans a game."

Terrell turns the corner and heads for the goal line. After a year on the bench, he became a starter for Georgia in 1993.

Georgia coach Ray Goff. He and Terrell rarely saw eye-to-eye.

Terrell's plan was to watch and learn during his first year at Georgia, then move into the starting line-up for his final two seasons. In 1992, he served as the backup for Garrison Hearst. When Hearst moved on to the National Football League (NFL) in 1993, Terrell became the first-string halfback. Georgia's team that year was not a strong one, and the Bulldogs were beaten by teams they had defeated in the past. Coach Goff began to blame Terrell. The coach had no complaint about his performance during games (in one game Terrell gained 177 yards!), but insisted that he should be practicing harder. Terrell did not like too much contact during workouts. He believed that light practices helped make him stronger on game day. He also was afraid that a big hit might trigger another one of his episodes. Coach Goff used Terrell less and less. "I have no idea why he didn't use me more," Terrell says. "I always thought I was capable in college, but that's the way he wanted to go."

Prior to the 1994 season, Terrell contacted his buddy, Jamaul. He had just been discharged from the Navy and was back home in San Diego. Terrell asked him to come to Georgia and stay with him. College was a lot of fun, not to mention a lot safer than their old neighborhood. Jamaul declined the offer, saying that he had gotten a job as an electrician's apprentice. Don't worry, he told Terrell, everything would be fine. A week later, Jamaul got into an argument with a man, who shot him dead. What else can go wrong, Terrell wondered.

⸻ ★ ★ ★ ⸻

He got his answer that summer, after he suffered a pulled hamstring during preseason practice. Terrell wanted to take it easy between games until his muscle healed. Coach Goff threatened to bench him if he did not practice. Terrell had no choice—he had to play. In a game against Tennessee, Terrell was running the ball when he felt the hamstring tear. The injury was severe enough to keep him out for a month, all but destroying any chance he had at being drafted by an NFL team. Although he did return to the lineup at season's end, Terrell's football career looked like it was over.

★ 4 ★

SIXTH-ROUND SENSATION

Every NFL team knew about Terrell Davis. During his second year at Georgia, pro scouts saw a lot of things they liked. But his senior season made him look like washout. Worse, during the scouting combines held prior to the draft, his times in the 40-yard dash were terrible. The only team with any interest in Terrell on draft day was the Denver Broncos. They saw Terrell's final college game, noticing that he did many of the little things that do not show up on the stat sheets. They saw Terrell's willingness to punish enemy tacklers. They also noticed the way he always seemed to stumble

forward for an extra yard or two after being surrounded by defenders. So the team selected him in the sixth round of the 1995 draft.

Terrell started training camp at the bottom of the Denver depth chart. Each week, however, he managed to move up a notch. He learned the playbook from cover to cover and did not make a single mistake. In an exhibition contest against the San Francisco 49ers, Terrell hit return man Tyronne Drakeford so hard that he flew backwards 15 feet! Coach Mike Shanahan knew he had "stolen" a special player in the draft. By the season's opening game, Terrell had not only made the team—he had won the starting job!

Terrell's rookie year in the NFL was simply spectacular. In 1995, he averaged 4.7 yards every time he carried the ball, leading the American Football Conference (AFC). He also caught 49 passes. In all, Terrell amassed 1,484 yards—1,117 on the ground and 367 through the air. He also proved to be an accomplished blocker. "I knew that because of my lack of speed, I had to compensate one way or another," says Terrell. "Catching the ball and blocking were two things I needed to do in order to play. I started to develop those skills in high school, and they helped me a little bit in college. Now they are my greatest assets."

Terrell's presence transformed the Denver offense. For years, the Broncos had relied on the passing arm of quarterback John Elway. But Elway was getting older, and could no longer dodge the blitzes opponents used to flush him out of the pocket. With Terrell in the backfield, defenders now had to hold their ground. A team could not risk sending its linebackers and safeties after Elway. He could easily hand the ball to Terrell, who could run for first downs all game long. On the other hand, when defenses paid too much attention to Terrell, Elway was free to pick his most open receiver and drill a perfect spiral into his waiting arms.

John Elway (right) hands off to Terrell. In 1996, the Broncos built their offense around this talented twosome.

In 1996, the team took a major step forward. Coach Shanahan built an offense that made the most of his two stars, and they rolled to the AFC Western Division title. Terrell established a new team record with 1,538 yards, leading the AFC. Only Barry Sanders of the Detroit Lions gained more yards. Both players were named NFL All-Pros.

Denver coach Mike Shanahan

On paper, it was a great second season for Terrell. But an incident in a game against the San Diego Chargers nearly ruined it. Terrell took a hard hit on his helmet, and he felt one of his migraines coming on. In college, he had learned how to dull their effects with medication and by eliminating certain foods from his diet. But he had never experienced a migraine during an actual game—not even back in his Pop Warner days. Now Terrell was scared that it might happen at a big moment during a big game. Or worse, during every game.

★ 5 ★

A SUPER SEASON

To Terrell's great relief, the 1997 season passed without a major migraine. He suffered a few episodes during the season, but always off the field. On the field, it was Terrell who was causing the headaches. He had become a complete NFL runner. Terrell could take a handoff, follow his blockers, and then wait for the defense to make its move. Then he would choose an opening and explode through it for a big gain. Terrell became especially good at cutting back against the flow of tacklers, which made opponents cautious about chasing him too aggressively.

Terrell makes one of his famous cut-back moves against the Kansas City Chiefs.

Elway, meanwhile, had the best year of his career. He tossed 27 touchdown passes and threw just 11 interceptions. Terrell scored 15 touchdowns, and once again led the AFC with 1,750 yards. The Broncos made the playoffs and defeated the Jaguars, Chiefs, and Steelers to earn a trip to the Super Bowl, with Terrell gaining over 100 yards in each game.

The Green Bay Packers were Denver's opponent in Super Bowl XXXII. Led by Brett Favre and Reggie White, the Packers were the defending champions and were favored to win again. Denver's strategy was to contain Favre and create special blocking schemes to free Terrell for big gains. In the first quarter, this

Terrell spies an opening in the Green Bay defense. Blocks like these enabled him to earn Super Bowl MVP honors.

---‎ ★ ★ ★ ---

strategy worked to perfection. The two teams traded touchdowns, and the Broncos turned a Packer turnover into a field goal for a 10–7 lead. A second Green Bay mistake gave Denver another excellent scoring chance. On the last play of the quarter, Elway handed the ball to Terrell deep in enemy territory, and he barreled toward the goal line. As Terrell was tackled, a Green Bay player accidentally hit him in the head with his knee.

The players walked down to the opposite end of the field to begin the second quarter, when Terrell began to lose his vision. His worst nightmare was coming true. He was having a migraine during the Super Bowl. Terrell veered over to the bench and told Coach Shanahan what was happening. Shanahan asked him if he could line up just one more time and pretend to take a handoff. Terrell said he could, as long as someone pointed him in the right direction. So on the very next play, Elway put the ball into

Terrell lets the world know who's number one, after Denver's victory over the Packers in Super Bowl XXXII.

Terrell's hand, then quickly pulled it out and hid it behind his leg. As the Packers piled on top of Terrell, Elway jogged untouched into the end zone!

Terrell left the game after that, not knowing if he would be able to return. He stayed out for the rest of the half, taking medication and breathing oxygen. By the beginning of the third quarter, he was ready to play again. To his relief, he felt fine. And for the rest of the game, he punished the Green Bay defense, slowly wearing it down. Terrell scored two more touchdowns, including the game-winner, with less than two minutes left. The Broncos were NFL champions, and Terrell was voted Super Bowl MVP.

BACK TO BACK

After 15 NFL seasons, John Elway finally had his championship ring. At the age of 37, he considered retiring from football. But the thought of returning and trying to win back-to-back Super Bowls was too tempting. As long as Terrell could continue pounding opponents and keeping pass rushers off his back, he was willing to give it a try.

Terrell knew he would have to carry more of the load than ever, so he spent the off-season working out to increase his strength and stamina. The result was an incredible year.

John Elway scans the field for receivers. Terrell was glad he came back for one final season.

In 1998, Terrell stomped opponents week after week, probing for weaknesses early in games, and then dominating in the third and fourth quarters. He finished with 2,008 yards, becoming just the fourth runner ever to reach the 2,000-yard mark. For his historic performance, Terrell was named the NFL's Player of the Year.

Terrell is one of just four players to gain 2,000 yards in a season. He was named the league's top player in 1998.

Terrell celebrates his second Super Bowl win. He kept the Falcons occupied while John Elway threw for 336 yards.

★ ★ ★

Once again, the Broncos rolled through the playoffs, defeating the Dolphins and Jets to earn a return trip to the Super Bowl. This time, their opponent was the Atlanta Falcons. Atlanta was coached by Dan Reeves, who had once been the coach of the Broncos. Reeves believed that Elway would not be able to beat the Falcons by himself, so he instructed his defenders to "take Terrell out of the game." The second part of the plan worked. The Falcons limited Terrell to just 103 yards. The first part, however, was a disaster. Elway picked the Atlanta defense apart, racking up 336 passing yards and putting the game out of reach in the third quarter. The final score was 34–19, but the Falcons never had a chance.

After the season, John Elway announced his retirement. The proud owner of two Super Bowl rings, he decided to walk away while he still could. There would be no more last-minute comebacks, no more long bombs, no more crazy headfirst dives for the goal line, and no more end-zone salutes. After attending Elway's tearful farewell, the Denver players knew it was time to turn to Terrell for leadership. The Broncos were "his team" now.

As the top player in his sport, Terrell can now look back and see how important it is to keep trying no matter how bad things seem. Few kids have had to endure what he did, and few athletes have had as many setbacks. "Don't give up," Terrell tells people who ask for his advice. "I say that with conviction. It happened to me. Don't ever give up."

Now he can focus on his future. Will it include more records? More championships? Or might it all end tomorrow? Whatever happens, Terrell will be all right with the final score. As long as he keeps playing, however, he does have one important goal. He wants fans to remember that he brought something special to the NFL. As he puts it, "I want to leave my signature on the game."

Whether or not Terrell realizes it, he has already accomplished that goal. If he were to quit tomorrow, he would rank among the most special people ever to step on a football field.

Terrell and Howard Griffith exchange the Bronco salute. With John Elway gone, Terrell is now the team's field general.

C★H★R★O★N

1972	• Oct. 28: Terrell is born in San Diego, California.
1988	• Terrell begins playing high-school football for Lincoln Prep.
1991	• Terrell plays for Long Beach State University, but the school decides to shut down its football program after his first year.
1992	• Terrell transfers to the University of Georgia.
1993	• Terrell becomes the starting halfback for the University of Georgia.
1995	• Drafted in the sixth round by the Denver Broncos, Terrell is runner-up to Curtis Martin as NFL Rookie of the Year.

O·L·O·G·Y

1996	• Terrell wins the AFC rushing title and is named to the NFL All-Pro team.
1998	• Terrell scores a record three touchdowns in the Super Bowl and is voted Super Bowl MVP. The Broncos beat the Packers, 31–24, in Super Bowl XXXII.
1999	• Terrell is named NFL Player of the Year and sets a record with his seventh straight 100-yard post-season game. The Broncos defeat Atlanta, 34–19, in Super Bowl XXXIII.

TERRELL DAVIS

Place of Birth **San Diego, California**
Date of Birth **October 28, 1972**
Height **5' 11"**
Weight **210 pounds**
Colleges **Long Beach St. & University of Georgia**
Pro Team **Denver Broncos**
All-Pro **1996, 1997, 1998**
MVP, Super Bowl **XXXII**
NFL MVP **1998**

STATISTICS

Season	Team	Carries	Yards	Catches	Yards	TDs
1995	Broncos	237	1,117	49	367	8
1996	Broncos	345*	1,538*	36	310	15
1997	Broncos	369	1,750*	42	287	15***
1998	Broncos	392	2,008**	25	217	23
Totals		1,343	6,413	152	1,181	61

* Led AFC
** Led NFL
*** Tied for NFL lead

ABOUT THE AUTHOR

Caleb MacLean is a sports researcher and writer who has worked on numerous books for children, including several titles in the Grolier All-Pro Biography series. He also has contributed to projects for Children's Television Workshop, ESPN, and The Walt Disney Company. A lifelong Cubs fan, Caleb now resides in Studio City, California. He has written two books in the Sports Stars series.